ASTRONAUT TRAVEL GUIDES

STARS and GALAXIES

ISABEL THOMAS

Heinemann
LIBRARY
Chicago, Illinois

www.capstonepub.com
Visit our website to find out
more information about
Heinemann-Raintree books.

To order:
☎ Phone 800-747-4992
🖳 Visit www.capstonepub.com
to browse our catalog and order online.

Edited by Nancy Dickmann and Laura Knowles
Designed by Steve Mead
Original illustrations © Capstone Global
   Library Ltd 2013
Picture research by Mica Brancic

Originated by Capstone Global Library Ltd
Printed and bound in the United States of
America in North Mankato, Minnesota.
112012   007034

16 15 14 13 12
10 9 8 7 6 5 4 3 2 1

**Library of Congress Cataloging-in-
   Publication Data**
Thomas, Isabel, 1980-
   Stars and galaxies / Isabel Thomas.—1st ed.
      p. cm.—(Astronaut travel guides)
   Includes bibliographical references and index.
   ISBN 978-1-4109-4573-0 (hb)—ISBN 978-1-
4109-4582-2 (pb) 1. Stars—Juvenile literature.
2. Galaxies—Juvenile literature. I. Title.
   QB801.7.T49 2013
   523.8—dc23   2011039069

Acknowledgements
We would like to thank the following for
permission to reproduce photographs: Corbis
p. 9 (© Stapleton Collection); European
Space Agency p. 34; Getty Images pp. 7
(The Bridgeman Art Library), 8 (Image Work/
amanaimagesRF); Mark Thompson pp. 5 bottom,
16; NASA p. 4, 5 middle and 37 (SOHO), 5
top, 13 (Glenn Image Gallery), 14, 15 (ESA,
Hubble Heritage Team), 18 (ESA, and The
Hubble Heritage Team (STScI/AURA)), 25 (ESA/
JPL/Arizona State Univ.), 27, 29 (JPL-Caltech),
30 (Marshall Space Flight Center/SAO/CXC),
31 (Marshall Space Flight Center/The Hubble
Heritage Team (STScI/AURA)), 32 (Daniel
Verschatse (Antilhue Observatory)), 33 (ESA, and
C.R. O'Dell (Vanderbilt University)), 38 (JHU/APL);
Robert Gendler p. 20; Science Photo Library
pp. 21 (David A. Hardy), 22 (Eckhard Slawik);
Serge Brunier p. 19; Shutterstock pp. 11
(© Mike Norton), 39 (© Rick Whitacre), 40-41
(© Martiin/Fluidworkshop).

Design image elements reproduced with
permission of Shutterstock/© Clearviewstock/
© Irina Solatges/© William Attard McCarthy.

Cover photograph of a spiral galaxy reproduced
with permission of Shutterstock/© Aquatic
creature.

We would like to thank Mark Thompson, Paolo
Nespoli, and the ESA for their invaluable help in
the preparation of this book.

Every effort has been made to contact copyright
holders of material reproduced in this book.
Any omissions will be rectified in subsequent
printings if notice is given to the publisher.

Disclaimer
All the Internet addresses (URLs) given in this
book were valid at the time of going to press.
However, due to the dynamic nature of the
Internet, some addresses may have changed,
or sites may have changed or ceased to exist
since publication. While the author and publisher
regret any inconvenience this may cause readers,
no responsibility for any such changes can be
accepted by either the author or the publisher.

CONTENTS

Some words are shown in bold,
like this. You can find out what they
mean by looking in the glossary.

DON'T FORGET

These boxes will remind you
what you need to take with
you on your big adventure.

NUMBER CRUNCHING

Don't miss these little
chunks of data as you speed
through the travel guide!

AMAZING FACTS

You need to know these
fascinating facts to get
the most out of your
space safari!

WHO'S WHO?

Find out about the space
explorers who have
studied the universe in
the past and today.

VISITING STARS AND GALAXIES

The ultimate astronaut's adventure is a trip to the most breathtaking and dangerous sights in the **universe**. From enormous explosions to mysterious glowing gases, this guide reveals the secrets of stars and galaxies.

star

galaxy

This photograph of the night sky was taken using a **telescope**. In the daytime, our nearest star—the Sun— outshines them all.

WHERE ARE THEY?

The Sun is our nearest star. This is why it looks so much bigger and brighter than other stars. It is close enough to be our main source of heat and light, and all life on Earth depends on it. It is a good place to start your trip.

Not all stars are like our Sun. To see the most amazing sights, you will need to visit other stars in our galaxy. The Sun is one of about 200 billion stars held together in a huge collection of stars, gas, and dust called the Milky Way.

For an even bigger adventure, you can travel beyond the Milky Way and explore other galaxies. There are hundreds of billions of galaxies in the universe, so you will have many great options.

See page 14 for a map of the skies and start planning your trip.

Find out what makes stars so scorching on pages 36–37.

Meet **astronomer** Mark Thompson on page 16.

NUMBER CRUNCHING

The distances between stars are so big that they are not measured in miles or kilometers. You will need to plan your journey in **light years**. One light year is the distance that light travels in one year. Light travels fast. It makes the 93-million-mile (150-million-kilometer) journey from the Sun to Earth in just 8 minutes.

EXPLORING STARS AND GALAXIES FROM EARTH

It is not just astronauts who are interested in stars and galaxies. Humans have been gazing at the night sky for thousands of years. Our knowledge of stars has changed over time—and so have the methods used to explore them.

CAVE CONSTELLATIONS

The earliest maps of the night sky are painted on cave walls. Star patterns painted in France's Lascaux caves are more than 17,000 years old. Ancient peoples imagined that they could see the figures of animals, people, and objects in the stars. They began to name groups of the brightest stars. A **constellation** is a group of stars joined up by imaginary lines to form a shape.

NUMBER CRUNCHING

In ancient times, there were no city lights to block the view of the stars. People would have been able to see up to 6,000 stars in the sky over the course of a year.

Ancient Egyptian paintings show the sky goddess, Nut, stretched across the sky and covered in stars.

Many ancient cultures linked the constellations to their religion. Early **astronomers** named stars and constellations after gods and goddesses. They created stories and **myths** to explain where these pictures came from. Our nearest star, the Sun, was often thought to be a god itself.

From Earth, groups of stars seem to move across the sky each night. Many early cultures used the position of stars and constellations like a calendar, to tell them when the seasons were changing. For example, the ancient Egyptians knew that when the bright star Sirius rose just before the Sun, the Nile River was about to flood. This helped them to plant and harvest crops at the right times.

THE ANCIENT GREEKS

From around 450 BCE, the ancient Greeks studied the constellations mapped by other people. They told their own myths and stories about these pictures in the sky and added new constellations of their own. Like other early peoples, the ancient Greeks did not know what stars really were. Greek **philosopher** Heraclitus thought that they were lit every night like oil lamps! However, they began naming and recording the movements of the brightest stars in the sky.

AMAZING FACTS

The constellation Orion is named after a great hunter who carried a bronze club. In Greek myths, Orion was killed by a scorpion. The scorpion-shaped constellation Scorpius is opposite Orion in the sky. Each night, Orion is said to run away below the **horizon** as Scorpius rises!

Orion can be seen from most parts of the world.

ARABIC ASTRONOMY

From the 600s CE, Arabic astronomers built huge **observatories** and better **instruments** to track the movement of stars across the sky. Eventually, Arabic astronomers such as Ulugh Beg (1394–1449) were able to create more accurate records of star positions.

Danish astronomer Tycho Brahe (1546–1601) became famous for the instruments he made in order to watch the skies. He kept records for more than 20 years, and his observations were the most accurate that had ever been made. Although his own ideas about the stars were wrong, his work led to many great discoveries.

Early astronomers imagined that stars were all the same distance from Earth, traveling in circles around our planet. They recorded the positions of the stars on globes.

SCIENTIFIC ASTRONOMY

New technology helped astronomers to discover what stars were like inside. When the telescope was invented in 1609, it was suddenly possible to make objects in the sky look many times bigger. Astronomy became more popular than ever, and hundreds of new observatories were built around the world. Astronomers raced to name stars that had been too faint to see before. They also noticed that there were different types of stars.

From the 1840s, astronomers began to photograph the images picked up by telescopes, instead of drawing everything they saw. Cameras can see much fainter objects than our eyes can. Better clocks also allowed astronomers to record the movements of stars more precisely. All these discoveries led to new ideas about how our planet and **solar system** began.

AMAZING FACTS

Unlike other stars, the North Pole star does not seem to move across the sky as Earth spins around. It stays in the same position all night. This allowed early sailors to find north and to figure out their **latitude** (how far from the equator they were).

SPLITTING LIGHT

In the 1860s, an exciting technique called spectroscopy allowed scientists to split starlight into its different colors and figure out what stars are made from. They discovered that stars are made from some of the same basic substances that are found on Earth. The next step was figuring out what happens to these materials inside stars to produce light and heat.

North Pole Star

This photograph was taken over a long time period. As Earth spins, the stars appear to move, leaving trails in the night sky. Unlike the other stars, the North Pole Star hardly seems to move at all.

THE SPACE AGE

In the 1900s, space scientists developed many new ways to study stars. These included spacecraft that can take telescopes and other instruments above Earth's **atmosphere**, to get a better look at space.

NUMBER CRUNCHING

The Hubble Space telescope **orbits** Earth 353 miles (569 kilometers) above the surface. It changed astronomy by letting scientists see stars, galaxies, and other objects in amazing detail. The most distant object spotted by Hubble is a galaxy 13.1 billion light years away.

EYES IN SPACE

Remotely controlled telescopes in space have made many amazing discoveries. They detect **radiation** that is blocked by Earth's atmosphere and beam their pictures back to Earth. The **European Space Agency (ESA) satellite** *Hipparcos* was the first space mission sent to measure the position of stars. Between 1989 and 1993, it recorded the position, movements, brightness, and color of 2.5 million stars.

DON'T FORGET

A radio telescope will help you to spot objects in space that are invisible to your eyes. They detect radio waves from very distant or faint objects. Radio telescopes helped scientists discover the large clouds of gas and dust between stars, where new stars are made.

This picture of the Cat's Eye **Nebula** was taken by the Hubble Space Telescope. The nebula is 3,000 light years from Earth.

WAVES AND RAYS

In addition to the light we can see, stars release other types of waves and rays, such as the UV waves that cause sunburn. Telescopes like Hubble have instruments that can spot these types of radiation. This helps scientists to "see" stars and galaxies in different ways.

NAVIGATING THE SKIES

Astronomers think there are around 100 sextillion stars in the universe (that's 100,000,000,000,000,000,000,000 stars). A sky map will come in handy when planning your trip! Today's maps of the stars are still based on the constellations spotted by ancient peoples.

The International Astronomical Union made an official list of 88 constellations in 1922. The constellations are used to divide the sky into 88 areas. When today's astronomers use names like Orion, Leo, and Draco, they mean the areas containing these constellations, rather than the shapes themselves.

DON'T FORGET

To point your spaceship in the right direction, you will need to learn how to read a star atlas. Modern star atlases use a few straight lines to join the main stars in a constellation and help astronomers spot them instantly.

In a star chart, the stars are drawn at different sizes to show how bright they are.

CAN I VISIT A CONSTELLATION?

Visiting every star in a constellation would take a very long time! The stars in a constellation only look close together because they lie in the same direction when seen from Earth. Most stars in a constellation are very different distances from Earth. For example, the stars that form the shape of Orion range from 500 to 2,000 light years away.

Some constellations include smaller patterns of stars called asterisms. The famous Big Dipper is an asterism—a part of the constellation Ursa Major (the Great Bear).

AMAZING FACTS

The brightest stars in the sky still have names given by ancient astronomers. Today, most stars are named by combining the name of the constellation they are in with a Greek or Roman letter or a number. These are like zip codes for stars!

INTERVIEW WITH AN ASTRONOMER

Mark Thompson has been an amateur astronomer for 20 years. He has also hosted television shows about stars and space, helping adults and young people to understand the night sky.

Q *What is your favorite constellation to look at?*

A I might say Ursa Major and the Big Dipper. The Big Dipper itself isn't a constellation, it's just a part of a big constellation called Ursa Major, which is the Great Bear. But the Big Dipper is what everyone recognizes as the thing you can use to find the direction of north. But you can also use it as a signpost to find loads of other constellations in the sky, because follow the curve of the stars in one direction and you come to one group of stars, you follow the line of stars in the bowl of the Big Dipper and that takes you to another group of stars. It's actually just quite a big, easy-to-recognize constellation. It's great for finding your way around the sky.

Q *If you could travel anywhere in the universe, where would you like to go, and what would you hope to find?*

A I'd probably pick the center of our galaxy because we believe at the center of our galaxy is a large black hole. We don't know, we believe. There's quite a lot of evidence to suggest that there is a large black hole at the center of our galaxy … I'd love to get up close and personal to a black hole and see what it is really like. I wouldn't want to get too close, though, I wouldn't want to get sucked in!

Q What is the coolest gadget that you've been able to work with in order to look at space?

A I would absolutely say that it's a smartphone. All through my life I've used star charts and all sorts of complicated bits of paper trying to work out where things are. But with smartphones, you can get applications for just a few dollars, which you hold up to the sky and they show you what's visible in the sky in that direction. And they're phenomenal! They're so cheap and easy to use!

If I were to choose an astronomical piece of equipment I've used that is incredible, it would have to be the Faulkes Telescope System. This has two telescopes, one set up in Hawaii and one set up in Australia. You can access it across the Internet, and schools can access it as well. It's brilliant because it's so easy to use.

Q What's the most exciting thing that you've been able to see so far in space?

A An asteroid that passed between the Earth and the Moon … to be able to calculate its position and point the telescope at the right place and then just wait and to see it pass across the field of view of the telescope was phenomenal. I think what was so special about it as well was that the calculations that I had to do to work out where it was in the sky came from astronomers 400 or 500 years ago.

Stars are not spread out evenly through space. They are held together in groups called galaxies. Scientists think there are hundreds of billions of galaxies in the universe.

DISCOVERING GALAXIES

Around 100 years ago, astronomers thought that all stars were part of one galaxy—the one that we are in. In the 1920s, bigger and better telescopes revealed that some of the objects that looked like nebulae (clouds of dust and gas) were actually separate galaxies.

WHO'S WHO?

French astronomer Charles Messier (1730–1817) was one of the first people to spot galaxies, although he didn't know it! He was searching for **comets** and wanted to rule other objects out. In the 1700s, he made a list of 110 "fuzzy bodies" that were not comets. Forty of these were galaxies.

Today, Messier's fuzzy bodies are named with the letter M and the number he gave them, such as the galaxy M81.

STARS STICK TOGETHER

A galaxy is a huge group of stars, gas, and dust, held together by **gravity**—a force that pulls all objects toward each other. Galaxies contain from just a few million stars to several trillion stars.

Our Sun is part of a galaxy called the Milky Way. If we could look at the Milky Way from a great distance, we would see a huge disc of stars. From Earth, we can only see part of it.

In ancient times, people thought the Milky Way (shown here) looked like a trail of spilled milk. In fact, it is a band of millions of stars stretching across the sky.

NEIGHBORING GALAXIES

If you make the journey out of the Milky Way, your next stop is likely to be the Large and Small Magellanic Clouds. These small galaxies are the Milky Way's neighbors in space.

ANDROMEDA

The Andromeda Galaxy is the closest large galaxy to the Milky Way. It is so bright that it was first spotted in the 900s CE, but for hundreds of years astronomers thought it was just a cloud of gas and dust. In 1923, Edwin Hubble realized that Andromeda was in fact a separate galaxy.

Edwin Hubble figured out that Andromeda is 2.5 million light years from Earth.

Andromeda is larger than the Milky Way. Its huge size means that it can pull in smaller galaxies and rip them apart. The bad news is that Andromeda and the Milky Way are moving toward each other. The good news is that even if they do collide, it will not happen for another 5 billion years!

U.S. astronomer Edwin Hubble (1889–1953) discovered in 1923 that there were galaxies outside the Milky Way. After spotting Andromeda, he found many more galaxies and sorted them into different groups, depending on their shape. His work changed the way we think about the universe, and the Hubble Space Telescope was named after him.

These are the four main galaxy shapes.

lenticular (shaped like the lens in a magnifying glass)

irregular (clouds of stars with no special shape)

elliptical (round, shaped like eggs or footballs)

spiral (a bright middle and two or more curved arms of stars)

WHAT ARE STARS?

Now you know where to find stars. But what can you expect when you visit one? Information collected by instruments on Earth and in space tells us what stars are like up close. These are the facts you need to know before you go.

Betelgeuse

Rigel

WHAT ARE STARS MADE OF?

Stars are huge balls of hot, glowing gas. At their center, the **pressure** and temperature are so high that **nuclear fusion reactions** happen. This releases huge amounts of **energy.** Some of this energy escapes into space as light, heat, and other types of radiation. When you visit different stars, you will discover that their surface temperatures, colors, and brightness are different.

Massive stars, such as Rigel, are the hottest and brightest. They often glow with a blue or white light. Older stars, such as Betelgeuse, are less hot and are yellow, orange, or red.

Sun's atmosphere

surface layer, where energy escapes into space (9,930 °F)

core, where nuclear fusion reactions happen (27 million °F)

Studying our Sun has helped scientists to figure out what goes on inside a star. Stars are made up of different layers of gas.

DON'T FORGET

The Sun is so bright that it is very dangerous to look directly at, even from 93 million miles (150 million kilometers) away on Earth. An astronaut planning to get close to a star will need special eye protection. Space helmets are lined with gold to protect astronauts' eyes.

LIFE AND DEATH OF STARS

Stars do not shine forever. When their supply of fuel runs out, their nuclear fusion reactions stop. The amount of fuel a star starts with determines how long a star lives and how it dies.

1. Like other stars, the Sun began life inside a swirling cloud of gas and dust called a nebula. A clump of gas and dust formed and grew larger and larger. Gravity pulled the material closer together.

2. The pressure and temperature at the center of the clump grew. When it got hot enough, nuclear fusion reactions started. Energy was released into space, and the Sun started to shine.

3. The new Sun burned brightly for millions of years. This is the stage our Sun is in now. As it gets older, its fuel will begin to run out and it will become less bright. A medium-sized star like our Sun shines for around 10 billion years. More massive stars use up their fuel more quickly, so they have shorter lives.

6. The white dwarf cools down and stops shining. It becomes a black dwarf and is almost invisible.

5. The material left behind will shrink to form a white dwarf. White dwarfs are about the size of a planet, but are very dense.

4. As the Sun's fuel runs out, the dying Sun will get bigger and become a red giant. Its outer layers of gas will start to escape into space.

This is the life cycle of a medium-sized star like our Sun.

SUPERNOVA

Stars that are around eight times bigger than our Sun die in a more dramatic way. After expanding into red supergiants, they explode! The enormous explosion is called a **supernova**. Gases and dust zoom away into space, leaving a small spinning star called a neutron star. A neutron star is much more **dense** than a white dwarf. A chunk of neutron star the size of a pinhead would weigh 100 times as much as the world's largest skyscraper!

The gas and dust that escape in a supernova glow brightly for thousands of years. They form wispy shapes, such as the Crab Nebula.

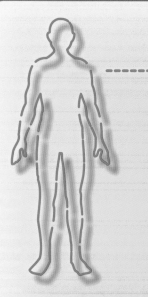

WHO'S GOING WITH YOU?

If you could put together a dream crew for your sightseeing tour of the stars, it might include some of the following people. Who do you think would be most useful to bring?

CREW MEMBERS:

Ejnar Hertzsprung (1873–1967) and
Henry Norris Russell (1877–1957)

Hertzsprung and Russell are famous for figuring out the relationships between a star's **mass**, color, temperature, and brightness. They can help you figure out what stage of life each star is experiencing.

POTENTIAL JOBS:

Star spotters

CREW MEMBER:

Nuclear fusion scientist

Scientists from different countries are working together to try to use controlled nuclear fusion reactions on Earth, as a source of energy. These fusion experts will know the hazards to look out for when visiting the universe's natural nuclear reactors.

POTENTIAL JOB:

Health and safety officer

CREW MEMBER:

Subrahmanyan Chandrasekhar (1910–1995)

Chandrasekhar won a Nobel Prize for his discoveries about the life and death of stars. He could help you find exciting events like supernovas.

POTENTIAL JOB:

Tour guide

CREW MEMBER:

Henrietta Swan Leavitt (1868–1921)

Leavitt had an amazing discovery that made it possible to figure out the distance of very distant stars. Her knowledge would help you to plan your journey.

POTENTIAL JOB:

Route planner

CREW MEMBER:

Sergei Krikalev (born 1958)

Krikalev holds the world record for the most time spent in space. His six missions lasted for a total of 803 days, 9 hours, and 39 minutes. He would have lots of ideas to help you cope on your long journey to the stars.

POTENTIAL JOB:

Mission specialist

TOP SIGHTS TO SEE

Stars may look similar from Earth, but get a little closer and you will discover some dazzling sights. From giant galaxies to shining supernovas, these are some of the famous features that you will see on your tour.

PROXIMA CENTAURI

Proxima Centauri is a great first stop, because it is the closest star to our Sun. This still means traveling for 4.2 light years without a break! Proxima Centauri is a small orange-red star that looks very dim from Earth. It can only be seen with a telescope, and it was not discovered until 1915. Watch out for Proxima's **flares**, which send sudden bursts of light and other types of radiation into space.

NUMBER CRUNCHING

The Milky Way is a large galaxy shaped like a disc with a bulge in the middle. The disc is 100,000 light years across and 2,000 light years thick. Our Sun is 25,000 light years from the center. The Milky Way is turning very slowly. It takes the Sun about 225 million years to go around the Milky Way once. The last time the Sun was in its current position, dinosaurs were walking on Earth.

MIRA

Mira is one of the most famous stars in the Milky Way. Every 330 days, it becomes incredibly bright. Then it slowly fades until it is invisible from Earth. The changing brightness is caused by temperature changes inside the star. Mira is a red giant that is losing its outer layers as it dies. In 2007, astronomers discovered that Mira has a huge tail, formed by the gas and dust it sheds as it hurtles through space. It is the first time a star with a tail has been seen!

Mira's amazing tail is more than 13 light years long! The star speeds along at around 80 miles (130 kilometers) per second.

SEEING DOUBLE

Star systems are groups of two or more stars that are held together by gravity. They offer a chance to see several stars in one trip!

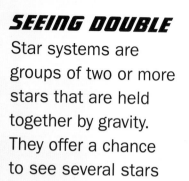

Sirius is the brightest star in the night sky. It is actually two stars that orbit each other.

HEADING NORTH

The North Pole Star (Polaris) is one of the best-known stars in our sky. Its position above the North Pole means that sailors could use it to find north before compasses and maps were invented. Until 1780, no one knew that Polaris is actually several stars!

Polaris A is a supergiant, and Polaris B is a smaller star, like our Sun. The stars are around 186 billion miles (300 billion kilometers) apart, but without a telescope they look like one star. In 2006, the powerful Hubble telescope allowed astronomers to see a third star in the Polaris system, a tiny dwarf star just 1.7 billion miles (2.8 billion kilometers) from Polaris A. There are thought to be two more objects in the system, but you will have to look for these when you get up close.

V838 Monocerotis is an unusual star that was discovered in 2002, when it suddenly became the brightest star in the Milky Way galaxy. A burst of energy had made it 600,000 times brighter than our Sun. Afterward, the star went back to normal. Astronomers still do not know why V838 Monocerotis became so bright. Did two stars crash into each other? Perhaps you will solve the mystery on your trip!

Months after V838 Monocerotis's burst of energy, the Hubble space telescope photographed these amazing shells of dust around the star. They are lit up by light from the explosion.

STAR NURSERIES

Some galaxies are home to **star nurseries**. These are dazzling areas where many new stars are being formed. Our nearest star nursery is the Orion Nebula, 1,500 light years away. But for the best photographs, head for the Tarantula Nebula, nearly 180,000 light years away in the Large Magellanic Cloud galaxy.

The Horsehead Nebula is a star nursery in the Milky Way. Do you think it looks like a horse's head?

DYING WITH STYLE

Dying stars create some of the most spectacular sights in the universe. Medium-sized stars like our Sun release clouds of gas and dust as they die. Gravity and **magnetic fields** can bend this escaping material into strange shapes. The closest example of this is the Helix Nebula. Comet-shaped "droplets" of gas surround a very hot star at the center. Each "droplet" is twice as wide as our solar system!

The clouds of gas and dust around dying stars are often named after objects they look like. Some of the strangest sights are the Cat's Eye Nebula, the Eskimo Nebula, and the Ant Nebula. There is even a nebula shaped like a hamburger!

The Helix Nebula is in the constellation of Aquarius. Amazing images of it can be seen using the Hubble Space Telescope.

When huge stars die in supernova explosions, their outer layers zoom off into space at great speeds. If you would like to see a supernova up close, visit Eta Carinae. This massive star is very unstable. Balloon-shaped clouds of gas are escaping from its sides. Astronomers expect the star to explode in the next million years.

INTERVIEW WITH AN ASTRONAUT

Paolo Nespoli is an Italian astronaut with the European Space Agency (ESA). He is also a qualified pilot, engineer, scuba diver, and parachute instructor. In 2007, Paolo went into space for 15 days, and in 2010 he spent 6 more months in space.

Q *If you could travel anywhere in the universe, where would you like to go, and what would you hope to find?*

A I would look for a planet somewhere that had more or less the same characteristics as Earth. I really believe that we are not alone in the universe. If you look at the amount of stars, or planets—we are talking about millions, if not billions of planets—it's impossible, in my opinion, that there are not planets that are similar to Earth. So, I would be curious about going farther away and discovering an Earth-like planet somewhere.

Q *Do you have a space hero? Someone from the history of space travel whom you really admire?*

A Yuri Gagarin. As a kid he was one of my heroes that I looked up to. Later on, I met several astronauts. For example, I met Pete Conrad, which was extremely nice. He was the commander of the second mission to the Moon. I met him several times, even before I was an astronaut, and it was a wonderful opportunity to talk to him.

When I was hired as an astronaut, I was transferred to **NASA's** Johnson Space Center. There was one of the Apollo astronauts there, named John Young. He would always have something to say and it was really interesting.

Q *Do you think there will ever be human colonies in space?*

A That's a good question. I would say in the future, I'm talking about 5,000 to 10,000 years from now … I would imagine us, as humans, to have achieved much higher technological and social goals. From space you can see that we are making a really big change in this planet, so we have to be careful what we are doing.

But I envision us going somewhere else, looking around, exploring. This is one of the traits that I think has kept us alive as a species: our curiosity, our incapability of being satisfied with what we have and always wanting more. I think if I look at all of this, I cannot help but picture ourselves somehow leaving this planet and going looking for another Earth or something like that.

COULD HUMANS REALLY VISIT STARS?

Although space scientists have mapped stars and photographed other galaxies, no human has ever been beyond our Moon. Could astronauts visit other stars or galaxies one day?

GETTING THERE

The nearest star outside our solar system is 4.2 light years away. Unless humans traveled close to the speed of light, they would die of old age before they got there. No power source could provide enough energy to make a spaceship go that fast.

EXTREME HEAT

Even visiting our closest star would be very difficult for a human. The temperature at the Sun's surface (the coolest part of the star) is 9,900 degrees Fahrenheit (5,500 degrees Celsius)—hot enough to boil almost every material on Earth.

NUMBER CRUNCHING

Spaceships that carry astronauts to the **International Space Station** have heat shields that can cope with temperatures up to 4,700 degrees Fahrenheit (2,600 degrees Celsius). This is the temperature around 1.3 million miles (2 million kilometers) from the Sun's surface.

Up close, the Sun is very unwelcoming. Earth is the perfect distance away for the Sun's heat and light to help living things, rather than destroy them.

SUCKED IN

If astronauts could protect themselves from deadly radiation and reach a star's surface, landing would be very difficult. Stars are not solid. They are made of very hot gas. There would be nothing to stop the Sun's gravity—28 times stronger than Earth's surface gravity—from pulling you down toward the center of the star.

FUTURE EXPLORATION

Humans may not be able to get close to stars, but that does not stop us from wanting to study them. Understanding stars and galaxies helps scientists to learn more about our planet.

SOLAR PROBE+

Space scientists have many questions about our closest star. They want to know why the energy it releases is always changing. They want to find out how these changes affect Earth. NASA is designing the first space probe that can fly into the Sun's fiery atmosphere, to answer some of these questions. *Solar Probe+* will travel around the Sun about 4.3 million miles (7 million kilometers) from its center.

Solar Probe+ will be around the size of a car. It will have a carbon shield to protect the instruments from temperatures of up to 3,600 degrees Fahrenheit (2,000 degrees Celsius).

SEEING RED

Space scientists have developed many ways to get a better look at stars. **Infrared** telescopes such as the ESA's Herschel Space Observatory and NASA's Spitzer Space Telescope detect infrared light released by stars. This helps them to spot cooler, fainter stars, such as brown dwarfs, and distant galaxies that are invisible to our eyes.

EXPLORING FROM THE GROUND

Although we cannot really rocket to the stars, thousands of new space discoveries are made from Earth every year. Some are even found by amateur astronomers. Hunt down your nearest public telescope and start your star-spotting mission with your feet firmly on the ground!

The Kepler space telescope is hunting for planets that orbit other stars. Planets do not release their own light, so they are very hard to spot. A planet similar to Earth may even have alien life!

Even if you cannot travel to the stars, you can still see amazing things if you watch the night sky.

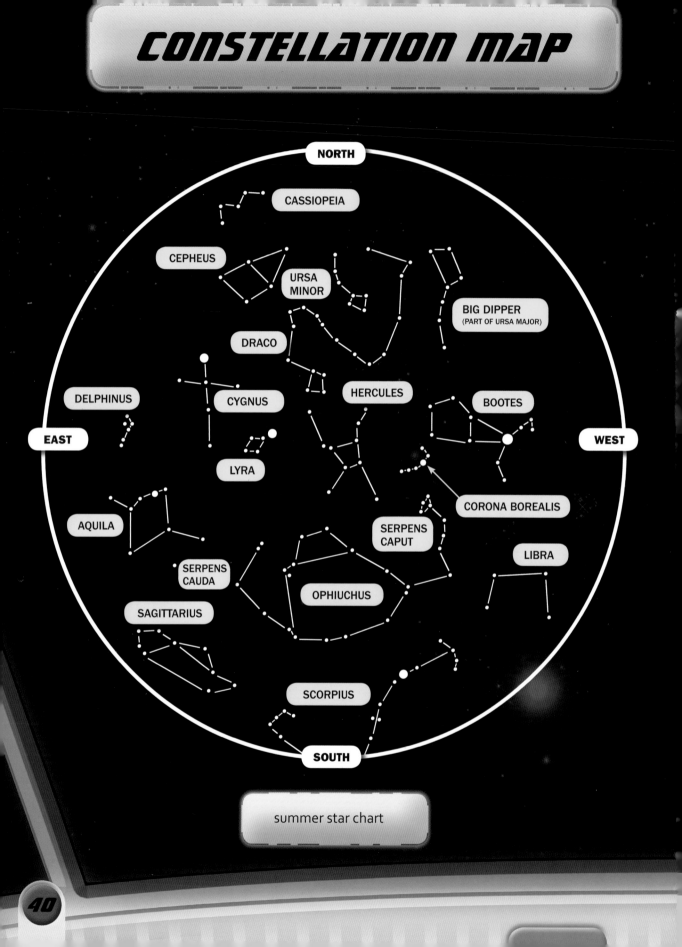

CONSTELLATION MAP

NORTH

CASSIOPEIA

CEPHEUS

URSA
MINOR

BIG DIPPER
(PART OF URSA MAJOR)

DRACO

DELPHINUS

CYGNUS

HERCULES

BOOTES

EAST

WEST

LYRA

CORONA BOREALIS

AQUILA

SERPENS
CAPUT

LIBRA

SERPENS
CAUDA

OPHIUCHUS

SAGITTARIUS

SCORPIUS

SOUTH

summer star chart

You can use these star charts to help you spot some of the main constellations in the night sky of the Northern Hemisphere. You will see different stars as the seasons change.

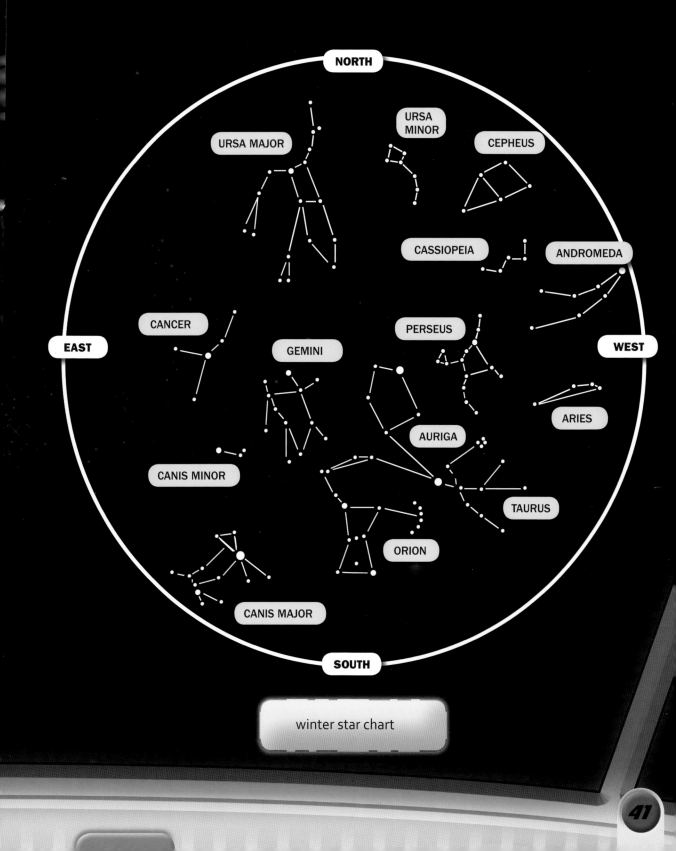

winter star chart

TIMELINE

around 150 BCE Greek astronomer Hipparchus invents the astrolabe, an instrument used to measure the position of bright stars and to estimate latitude.

1054 CE Chinese astronomers see a supernova explosion so bright it can be seen during the day.

1428 Arabic astronomer Ulugh Beg builds a large observatory that will go on to record the position of more than 1,000 stars.

1603 Johann Bayer begins to use Greek letters to name stars, a system that is still used today.

1609 Astronomer Galileo Galilei is the first person to use a telescope to study space, and he sees the Milky Way galaxy.

1668 Isaac Newton invents the reflecting telescope, which gives a much better image of stars.

1781 Messier spots many new objects, including galaxies, while he is looking for comets, but he does not realize what they are.

1904 California's Mount Wilson Observatory is set up specifically to study the Sun.

1923 Hubble discovers that there are other galaxies beyond the Milky Way.

1937 The first radio telescope is built, giving astronomers a new way to study very distant stars and galaxies.

1990 The Hubble Space Telescope is put into space, giving astronomers a better view of stars and galaxies.

1992 The first planet orbiting another star is discovered.

2003 The Spitzer infrared space telescope is launched, to monitor faint stars that are forming.

2009 The Kepler Space Telescope begins to monitor 100,000 stars, to find out how many have planets of their own.

2010 Scientists discover a "monster star" about 265 times bigger than the Sun, making it the biggest star ever found.

FACT FILE

When you visit different stars, you will discover that their surface temperatures, colors, and brightness vary. Massive stars are the hottest and brightest. They often glow with a blue or white light. Cooler stars are yellow, orange, or red.

Star color	Temperature	Example
Blue	72,000–52,200 °F (40,000–29,000 °C)	Orionis
Bluish white	50,500–17,500 °F (28,000–9,700 °C)	Rigel
White	17,300–13,000 °F (9,600–7,200 °C)	Sirius
Yellowish white	12,800–10,500 °F (7,100–5,800 °C)	Canopus
Yellow	10,300–8,500 °F (5,700–4,700 °C)	Sun
Orange	8,300–6,000 °F (4,600–3,300 °C)	Aldebaran
Red	5,800–3,800 °F (3,200–2,100 °C)	Betelgeuse

GLOSSARY

astronomer person who studies space

atmosphere layer of gases surrounding a planet

comet small object made up of ice and dust that orbits the Sun

constellation group of stars seen from Earth, joined by imaginary lines to make a figure, or one of 88 official areas of Earth's sky

dense made of tightly packed material

energy capacity to do work

European Space Agency (ESA) European organization involved in space research and exploration

flare sudden burst of energy released from a star into space

gravity force that pulls objects toward each other. Big objects such as planets have much stronger gravity than smaller objects, such as people.

horizon line where Earth's surface appears to meet the sky

infrared type of radiation given out by hot objects, including stars

instrument machine or tool for measuring something— for example, speed, temperature, or position

International Space Station large spacecraft orbiting Earth, where astronauts from different countries live and work

latitude measure of how far a place on Earth's surface is from the equator

light year unit used to make it easier to measure large distances. One light year is equal to 6 trillion miles— the distance that light travels in a year.

magnetic field region around a magnet where it has an effect on magnetic materials and other magnets

mass amount of material that makes up an object

myth traditional story, linked with a culture or religion

NASA short for "National Aeronautics and Space Administration," the U.S. space agency

nebula (more than one: **nebulae**) cloud of dust and gas in space

nuclear fusion reaction reaction in which two atoms join together to form a larger atom, releasing lots of energy

observatory building with telescopes and other instruments for observing (looking at) stars and planets

orbit path of an object around a star or planet

philosopher person who has studied philosophy and tries to answer difficult questions such as, "Why do we exist?"

pressure pushing force on an object from something touching it, such as the pushing force of the air on our bodies

radiation waves or particles that carry energy from one place to another. Light is one type of radiation.

satellite object, often human-made, that orbits a larger object. Human-made satellites carry instruments that gather information or send and receive radio signals.

solar system the Sun, the planets, and other objects that are in orbit around the Sun

star nursery bright area of space where many new stars are being formed

supernova huge explosion that happens when a giant star dies

telescope instrument that makes distant objects look bigger

universe everything that exists, including all of space and all the objects and energy in it

FIND OUT MORE

BOOKS

Bond, Peter. *DK Guide to Space* (DK Guides). New York: Dorling Kindersley, 2006.

Goldsmith, Mike. *Solar System* (Discover Science). New York: Macmillan, 2010.

Graham, Ian. *What Do We Know About the Solar System?* (Earth, Space, and Beyond). Chicago: Raintree, 2011.

Lippincott, Kristen. *Astronomy* (Eyewitness). New York: Dorling Kindersley, 2008.

APPS

Download **Star Walk**, hold a smartphone or tablet computer up to the night sky, and it will tell you exactly what you are looking at! Available from iTunes.

INTERNET SITES

FactHound offers a safe, fun way to find internet sites related to this book. All of the sites on FactHound have been researched by our staff.

Here's all you do:

Visit *www.facthound.com*

Type in this code: 9781410945730

PLACES TO VISIT

Hayden Planetarium
Central Park West and 79th Street, New York, N.Y. 10024
www.haydenplanetarium.org

Kennedy Space Center
SR 405, Kennedy Space Center, Florida 32899
www.nasa.gov/centers/kennedy

Smithsonian National Air and Space Museum
Independence Ave. at 7th St. SW, Washington, D.C. 20560
www.nasm.si.edu

FURTHER RESEARCH

Here are some starting points for finding out more about stars and galaxies:

- Find out more about the Kepler mission to hunt for other stars with planets at kepler.nasa.gov.
- See what you can find out about the different constellations.

WARNING

Make sure that you never look directly at the Sun. Although you can look at stars through binoculars or a telescope, you must never use these to look at the Sun. Looking at the Sun can damage your eyes.

INDEX